SMOOTHIES

A collection of delicious easy-to-make recipies

Contents

Originally published in 2007 by L&K Designs. This edition published in 2010 by Myriad Books Limited.

PRINTED IN CHINA

Publishers Disclaimer

The recipes contained in this book are passed on in good faith but the publisher cannot be held responsible for any adverse results. Please be aware that certain recipes contain nuts.

Smoothie Basics

A smoothie is a delicious and nutritious drink made up of blended fruit and or vegetables. Traditionally, smoothies are considered healthy drinks as the basic ingredients are typically packed with the vitamins and nutrients needed to maintain a healthy balanced diet, and in their most basic form they are an excellent way of ensuring that we eat lots of fruit and vegetables. They are also a great way of making sure that kids receive essential nutrients, as many smoothies look pretty yummy when made - not unlike milkshakes!

Over the past decade, fruit smoothies in particular have become an extremely popular choice, whether it be to replace a full meal, to help maintain a balanced diet or as a mid-afternoon snack. So much so that there is a multi-million pound industry that has grown from essentially one man's desire to create a healthy drink. Stephen Kuhnau, the founder of Smoothie King, claims to have created the original "smoothie" in the late 1960s, as a nutritional non-dairy drink (he suffered from dairy intolerance). Today, the smoothie industry has grown so fast that many of our highstreet stores have created their own smoothie ranges, in addition to the many independent cafes and chains that also offer the drinks. Yet, whilst these shop bought smoothies are unquestionably "convenient" they can be very expensive and also hide ingredients that are not necessarily as healthy or as good for you as you may think.

By creating your own smoothies, you may have to invest a little time, but you will in the long term save yourself money - even if you have to buy equipment to begin with. And for those times when you fancy something that is naughty as well as nice we have included a few indulgent recipes - and even a few that contain alcohol (these are clearly marked). To grab a smoothie on the go, make them up ahead of time. You can freeze a smoothie and thaw it out when you want it. You'll need to allow some space in the container because your smoothie will likely expand when freezing.

The only equipment that you really need to make a smoothie is a blender. Smoothie making is very simple, but here are some tips and ideas to keep in mind. The first step in making a smoothie is assembling your ingredients and there are four different categories of ingredients that you can use:

1. Liquids

These help to give your smoothie a thinner, drinkable consistency. Add the liquids to the blender first, to prevent it from binding up on the frozen fruit and getting stuck.

Fruit Juice: Any fruit juice works great; try squeezing the juice of an orange for a fresh flavour.

Milk: Using skim milk or soy milk adds protein and a creamy flavour and is also a healthier option than full fat milk.

Water: Plain water is sometimes the best option, especially if you have a lot of flavours going on with the other ingredients.

2. Fruits or Vegetables

The recipes don't always specify, but if you have time to freeze your fruit beforehand, your smoothie will stay colder and be thicker than if your fruit was warm. Large fruits (like bananas or melons) should be chopped into pieces before freezing. Spread the pieces on a plate or baking sheet while in the freezer which will make sure the fruit doesn't freeze in one big unmanageable lump. Once frozen, then you can store them together in a freezer bag or container. Using frozen strawberries, blueberries, or even mixed berries will add a sweet and slightly tart flavour.

3. Solid ingredients

These often make up the bulk of your smoothie, and for this category you will often have more than one of the following:

Yoghurt: Plain yoghurt is ideal if you are adding in your own fruit, since the fruit-infused yoghurts have hidden added sugars.

Fresh Fruits: Any fresh fruit — peaches, pears, mangos, and more — can be added to a smoothie; just remove any seeds and skin and toss into the blender.

Tofu: A smoothie with tofu will have added protein, which is important especially if you are drinking the smoothie for a meal; choose the silken kind as it is much creamier than the firm varieties.

Peanut Butter: This will add healthful fats and protein and great flavour, especially delicious with bananas.

4. Flavour Add-ins

These can pull all the flavours in the smoothie together and provide a "kick"; as an added bonus, the following also add a nutritional punch:

Cinnamon: Any spice, including cinnamon, can add flavour as well as boost the nutritional properties of your smoothie.

Ginger: Either freshly grated or powdered ginger will add a great spicy flavour to the smoothie. This works great with pineapple.

Mint: Fresh herbs such as mint or parsley give smoothies a fresh flavour. Just give a rough chop before tossing into the blender.

Nutritional Values of Fruits

Food	energy	water	fibre	fat	protein	sugar	vit.A
substance = 100 g.	kJ/Kcal	%	g	g	g	g	ug
Apple	207/49	84	2.3	0	0.4	11.8	2
Apricot	153/36	87	2.1	0	1.0	8.0	420
Avocado	523/126	81	0.2	10	2.0	7.0	20
Banana	375/88	76	2.7	0	1.2	20.4	3
Blackberry	170/40	85	8.7	0	2.0	8.0	30
Blueberry	204/48	80	8.4	0	1.0	11.0	0
Carrots	48 /11	92	3.3	0	0.6	2.2	312
Cherry	221/52	86	1.2	0	0.0	13.0	40
Cranberry	68 /16	89	4.2	0	0.0	4.0	0
Date	1275/300	20	7.5	0	2.0	73.0	0
Fig	340/80	80	2.0	0	1.0	19.0	10
Gooseberry	170/40	88	3.2	0	1.0	9.0	0
Grapefruit, Red	128/30	90	1.4	0	0.9	6.6	0
Grapes	274/64	83	2.2	0	0.6	15.5	0
Guava	306/72	81	5.3	0	1.0	17.0	30
Kiwi Fruit	168/40	84	2.1	0	1.1	8.8	5
Lemon	51/12	96	1.8	0	0.0	3.0	0
Lime	156/37	91	0.3	0	0.0	7.0	0
Lychee	323/76	82	1.5	0	1.0	18.0	0
Mandarin/Tangerine	177/42	88	1.9	0	0.9	9.5	12
Mango	255/60	84	1.0	0	0.0	15.0	210
Melon, Red Water	153/36	93	0.6	0	1.0	8.0	30
Melon, Cantaloupe	122/29	89	0.6	0	0.9	6.3	7
Orange	198/47	87	1.8	0	1.0	10.6	2
Papaya	136/32	91	0.6	0	0.0	8.0	40
Passion Fruit	158/37	88	3.3	0.4	2.6	5.8	125
Peach	151/36	89	1.4	0	1.0	7.9	15
Pear	201/47	86	2.1	0	0.3	11.5	0.0
Red Bell Pepper	119/28	91	2.2	0	1.0	6.0	172
Pineapple	211/50	84	1.2	0	0.4	12.0	20
Pomegranate	343/81	82	3.4	0	1.0	17.0	10
Plum	177/42	84	2.2	0	0.8	9.6	18
Strawberry	99/23	91	2.2	0	0.7	5.1	10
Tomato	48/11	97	1.4	0	0.9	1.9	140

Source: Nevo table 1996, Nevo Foundation, Netherlands Nutrition Centre

Nutritional Values of Fruits

Food substance = 100 g.	vit.C mg	vit.B1 mg	vit.B2 mg	vit.B6 mg	vit.E mg
Apple	15	0.02	0.01	0.05	0.5
Apricot	5	0.06	0.05	0.06	0.5
Avocado	17	0.06	0.12	0.36	3.2
Banana	10	0.04	0.03	0.36	0.3
Blackberry	150	0.08	0.04	0.07	1.0
Blueberry	10	0.02	0.03	0.05	1.9
Carrots	2	0.03	0.04	0.08	0.2
Cherry	10	0.02	0.02	0.04	0.1
Cranberry	15	0.00	0.01	0.07	0
Date	0	0.05	0.10	0.10	0.7
Fig	3	0.06	0.05	0.11	0
Gooseberry	30	0.02	0.01	0.08	0.4
Grapefruit, Red	40	0.07	0.02	0.03	0.5
Grapes	3	0.03	0.01	0.08	0.6
Guava	218	0.04	0.04	0.14	0
Kiwi Fruit	70	0.01	0.02	0.12	1.9
Lemon	40	0.06	0.02	0.04	0.8
Lime	140	0.03	0.02	0.08	0
Lychee	39	0.05	0.05	0	0
Mandarin/Tangerine	30	0.08	0.03	0.084	0.4
Mango	53	0.05	0.06	0.13	1.0
Melon, Red Water	6	0.04	0.05	0.07	0
Melon, Cantaloupe	32	0.05	0.02	0.10	0.2
Orange	49	0.07	0.03	0.06	0.1
Papaya	46	0.03	0.04	0.04	0
Passion Fruit	123	0.03	0.12	0	0.5
Peach	7	0.01	0.02	0.02	0.0
Pear	4	0.01	0.01	0.02	0.1
Red Bell Pepper	80	0.04	0.14	0.43	6.4
Pineapple	25	0.07	0.02	0.09	0.1
Pomegranate	7	0.05	0.02	0.31	0
Plum	5	0.02	0.03	0.10	0.7
Strawberry	60	0.02	0.03	0.06	0.4
Tomato	15	0.05	0.02	0.08	0.7

Spoons to millilitres

1/2 Teaspoon	2.5ml	1 Tablespoon	15ml
1 Teaspoon	5ml	2 Tablespoons	30ml
1-1/2 Teaspoons	7.5ml	3 Tablespoon	45ml
2 Teaspoons	10 ml	4 Tablespoons	60ml

Grams to Ounces

10g	0.25oz	225g	8oz
15g	0.38oz	250g	9oz
25g	1oz	275g	10oz
50g	2oz	300g	11oz
75g	3oz	350g	12oz
110g	4oz	375g	13oz
150g	5oz	400g	14oz
175g	6oz	425g	15oz
200g	7oz	450g	16oz

Metric to Cups

Description	Metric	Cup
Flour etc	115g	1 cup
Clear Honey etc	350g	1 cup
Liquids	225ml	1 cup

Liquid measures

Fl oz	Pints	ml
5fl oz	1/4 pint	150ml
7.5fl oz		215ml
10fl oz	1/2 pint	275ml
15fl oz		425ml
20fl oz	1 pint	570ml
35fl oz	1-3/4 pints	1 litre

Apple and Apricot Smoothie (serves 2)

Ingredients

1 apple, peeled, cored & chopped into small pieces
100g/3 1/2oz apricot halves (from a can) chopped
Syrup from can of apricot halves
200g/7oz natural yoghurt
Squeeze of lime juice
3 ice-cubes
1/2 teaspoon vanilla essence
Small pinch of sugar
2 tablespoon honey

Method

Place all ingredients in the blender, then blend for approximately 25 seconds or until smooth. Serve.

Apple and Avocado Smoothie (serves 2)

Ingredients

1 apple
1/2 ripe avocado
1/2 apple juice
3 ice cubes
3 sprigs mint leaves
1 teaspoon freshly squeezed lime juice

Method

Core and cut the apple into 4 pieces then combine all the ingredients together in a blender.

Apple and Banana Smoothie (serves 1)

Ingredients

110ml/1/2 cup of pure orange juice
55ml/1/4 cup low fat milk
1 whole banana, chopped into 4 pieces
1 whole apple, peeled and chopped into 4 pieces

Method

Place all ingredients in the blender for approximately 20 seconds.

Apple, Banana, Carrot and Orange Smoothie (serves 1)

Ingredients

1 apple, large, sweet
1 banana, large, ripe
1 carrot, large
1 orange, large
3 dates, pitted
1 tablespoon flax seed, whole, raw
6 ice cubes

Method

Blend together the apple, banana, carrot and orange. Add the dates, flax seed and the ice. Cover the blender and blend at high speed until smooth.

Apple & Blackberry Smoothie (serves 2)

Ingredients

200ml/3/4 cup apple juice, chilled
200g/3/4 cup greek yoghurt, chilled
1 tablespoon clear honey
250g/2 cups fresh blackberries
extra yoghurt and blackberries to serve, optional

Method

Place the apple juice, yoghurt, honey and blackberries in the goblet. Blend for approximately 20 seconds. Place a spoonful of yoghurt in the base of 2 serving glasses and add a few blackberries then add the smoothie and serve.

Apple Bliss Smoothie (serves 1)

Ingredients

1 apple
3 large strawberries
1 handful of grapes (red or green)
110ml/1/2 cup of apple juice

Method

Peel and chop apple into 4 pieces, add to blender. Next add the grapes, strawberries and apple juice and blend for approximately 40 seconds.

Apple and Blueberry Smoothie (serves 2)

Ingredients

300ml/1 1/3 cup semi-skimmed milk
1/2 apple
30g/1/4 cup of blueberries
115g/1 cup of black grapes
3 ice cubes

Method

Chop up the apple in to pieces, then place the rest of the ingredients in the blender then blend until smooth.

Apple Burst Smoothie (serves 2)

Ingredients

2 sliced apples
1 banana
1/2 tub of low fat natural yoghurt
225ml/1 cup of orange or apple juice
1 handful of mixed berries

Method

Take out the apple cores, chop into 4 segments, then chop banana into 4 pieces. Next, add all ingredients to the blender, blend for approximately 35 seconds.

Apple and Cherry Smoothie (serves 2)

Ingredients

1 apple
approx. 20 cherries
1 banana
1 kiwi
1 handful of blueberries
cloudy apple juice

Method

Stone the cherries and put into the blender. Add the chopped apple, banana, kiwi and blueberries. Blend with a generous splash of apple juice to loosen.

Apple and Cinnamon Smoothie (serves 2)

Ingredients

225ml/1 cup milk
225g/1 cup vanilla yoghurt
1 small apple
1/2 teaspoon ground cinnamon
handful of ice cubes

Method

Wash and peel apple. Remove seeds, and cut into cubes. Add all ingredients to the blender, and blend for one minute.

Apple and Coconut Smoothies (serves 2)

Ingredients

1 tablespoon of coconut milk
1/2 banana, chopped into cubes
55ml/1/4 cup of apple juice
1/4 teaspoon of fresh ginger root
2 small ice cubes or 1/2 cup crushed ice

Method

Add all ingredients to blender and process until smooth.

Apple and Cucumber Smoothie (serves 2)

Ingredients

1 apple
10 good thick slices of cucumber

Method

Place the sliced cucumber to the blender, next peel and cut the apple into 4 pieces and add this to the blender. Blend for approx 30 seconds and serve.

Apple and Grape Juice Smoothie (serves 1)

Ingredients

1 apple
110ml/1/2 cup of grape juice
200ml/! cup raspberry yoghurt
juice of 1 orange
a few handfuls of frozen berries
225ml/1 cup of milk

Method

Blend the apple, grape juice, yoghurt, berries and orange juice for about 30 seconds. Then add the milk and serve chilled or over ice.

Apple and Mango Smoothie (serves 1)

Ingredients

1/2 fresh mango (you could also use mango juice)
1 apple
110ml/1/2 cup yoghurt
1 dessert spoon runny honey

Method

Peel and core the apple and mango. Put the fruit into a blender with the yoghurt and honey and whiz for 20-30 seconds until really smooth.

Apple and Peach Smoothie (serves 1)

Ingredients

1 small apple
100g/1 cup peach halves (from a can) chopped
syrup from can of peach halves
200g/3/4 cup natural yoghurt
3 ice cubes
1/2 teaspoon vanilla essence
small pinch of sugar
2 tablespoon honey

Method

Place all ingredients in the blender, then blend for approximately 25 seconds or until smooth.

Apple and Pear Smoothie (serves 1)

Ingredients

1 tablespoon mixed seeds (sesame, sunflower, or flaxseed)
1 small apple
1 small ripe pear
150ml/3/4 cup of milk
vanilla extract (few drops)

Method

Blend all ingredients together for about 30 seconds or until you have reached the required consistency. If the smoothie is too thick add additional liquids to taste.

Apple and Raspberry Smoothie (serves 2)

Ingredients

3 apples (whichever type you prefer)
14 frozen raspberries
1 mango
1 medium-sized cup of apple juice

Method

Chop the apple and mango into chunks then place in the blender. Next add apple juice and mix for 1 minute. Finally, add raspberries and smooth for approximately 30 seconds.

Apple, Rhubarb, Berry and Honey Smoothie (serves 2)

Ingredients

1 carton of apple juice (1 litre or 1 quart)
4-5 stalks rhubarb, cut up
Stew the rhubarb in the apple juice until soft, about 10-15 minutes.

225ml/1 cup stewed rhubarb and juice
115g/1 cup fresh or frozen red berries
8 tablespoons plain yoghurt
1 tablespoon honey

Method

Combine 225ml/1 cup of the stewed rhubarb and apple juice in a blender with the remaining ingredients and blend until smooth.

Apple and Strawberry Smoothie (serves 1)

Ingredients

1 apple
150g/5oz strawberries

Method

Cut up the apple and the strawberries and put them in the blender. Blend until desired consistency, then pour into a glass with a strawberry on a cocktail stick for decoration.

Apple & Vanilla Smoothie (serves 2)

Ingredients

2 sliced apples
150ml/3/4 cup of apple juice
2 scoops of vanilla ice cream
2 ice cubes
crushed vanilla pod or vanilla extract (optional)

Method

Add all ingredients to blender and process until smooth.

Apple Zing (serves 2)

Ingredients

2 apples
1 medium can of pineapples in juice
12 ice cubes
2 tablespoons of fresh orange juice

Method

Add all ingredients to blender and blend until smooth. Serve and enjoy.

Create your own apple smoothie recipes and write them here:-

Name

Ingredients

Method

Name

Ingredients

Method

Name

Ingredients

Method

Banana Smoothie (serves 3)

Ingredients

55ml/1/4 cup orange juice
4 bananas
3 scoops of plain ice cream
2 tablespoons of golden syrup
3 tablespoons of plain yoghurt
lemon juice (optional)
sugar (optional)

Method

Cut the bananas into small pieces and put in the blender. Add all the other ingredients. Blend on full for 20 seconds. Put lemon juice around the rim of the glasses then roll the rim in the sugar so it sticks to the lemon juice.

Banana and Apple Smoothie (serves 1)

Ingredients

1 whole banana, chopped into 4 pieces
1 whole apple, peeled and chopped into 4 pieces
110ml/1/2 cup of pure orange juice
55ml/1/4 cup low fat milk

Method

Place all ingredients in the blender for approximately 20 seconds.

Banana Berry Smoothie (serves 2)

Ingredients

1 banana
110g/1/2 cup of low fat vanilla yoghurt
60g/1/2 cup of frozen peaches
115g/1 cup of frozen strawberries
1 tablespoon of orange juice concentrate

Method

Roughly chop the banana, then place all ingredients in the blender, (add ice if preferred to fill blender), blend until smooth.

Banana & Blackberry Smoothie (serves 2)

Ingredients

2 chopped bananas
200ml/7/8 cup milk
200g/3/4 cup Greek yoghurt, chilled
1 tablespoon clear honey
250g/2 cups fresh blackberries
Extra banana, yoghurt and blackberries to serve, optional

Method

Blend all of the ingredients together for approximately 20 seconds. Place a spoonful of yoghurt in the base of 2 serving glasses and add a few blackberries and slices of banana then add the smoothie and serve.

Banana Blitz Smoothie (serves 2)

Ingredients

1 banana
115g/1 cup of frozen strawberries
1 banana
6 ice cubes
banana essence flavouring

Method

Put strawberries, banana (chopped) and ice into the blender. Blend for approx 30 seconds. Then add a dash of banana flavouring (any kind) and blend until smooth.

Banana and Blueberry Smoothie (serves 2)

Ingredients

60g/1/2 cup of blueberries
1 banana
2 tablespoons of vanilla yoghurt
110ml/1/2 small cup of milk (skimmed or full fat)
1 scoop of vanilla ice cream

Method

Place all ingredients in the blender, mix for 30 seconds or till smooth.

Banana Boogie Smoothie (serves 2)

Ingredients

1 medium sized banana
honey flavoured yoghurt (add according to taste)
2 teaspoons honey
1/2 mug of milk

Method

Place all ingredients into a blender (leave a couple of slices of banana for later). Mix for 10 seconds at low speed, then mix again for 5 seconds at high speed. Serve into glasses and put the banana slices which you left to one side on the rim of each glass. Serve, drink and enjoy.

Banana Breakfast Smoothie (serves 2)

Ingredients

2 peaches
2 bananas chopped
225g/8oz can of crushed/chopped pineapple
75ml/1/3 cup of chopped mango
225ml/1 cup of low fat milk

Method

Place all ingredients into a blender, then blitz till smooth.

Banana Burst Smoothie (serves 1)

Ingredients

1 chopped banana
1 medium sized cup of any berry (strawberry/raspberry etc)
1 egg white
1 tablespoon of honey
1/2 small cup of any yoghurt (natural is good)
6 ice cubes

Method

Add all ingredients into blender and blend until smooth. Serve and enjoy.

Banana and Cherry Smoothie (serves 2)

Ingredients

1 banana, chopped into 4
130g/1 cup of sweet cherries (pitted and stem removed)
juice from 1/2 lemon
110g/1/2 cup of low-fat plain yoghurt
5 cubes of ice
2 drops of almond extract (optional)

Method

Put all ingredients in the blender and blend until smooth. Should you require a hint of almond, then add the drops of almond extract.

Bananarama Chocoholic Smoothie (serves 2)

Ingredients

1 banana
2 good scoops of chocolate ice cream
6 squares of milk or dark chocolate
150ml/2/3 cup of milk

Method

Chop the banana into four pieces then add to the blender. Then add the remaining ingredients, blend until desired consistency, pour into glasses and serve.

Banana and Chocolate Smoothie (serves 2)

Ingredients

1 banana
1 tablespoon chocolate syrup
1 medium cup of milk
1 medium cup of crushed ice

Method

Chop the banana into four pieces then add to the blender. Then add the chocolate syrup, milk and crushed ice. Blend until smooth. Pour into glasses and serve.

Banana and Chocolate Liqueur Smoothie (serves 2)

Ingredients (Alcoholic)

2 chopped bananas
2 scoops of chocolate ice cream
60ml/4 tablespoonsIrish Cream liqueur
2 teaspoons of instant coffee
55ml/1/4 pint of milk
8 ice cubes
chocolate sauce to decorate

Method

Crush ice, add bananas, milk, instant coffee, liqueur and ice cream to the blender, blend until smooth. Pour into two tall glasses decorated with the chocolate sauce, enjoy!

Banana and Coconut Smoothie (serves 2)

Ingredients

1 tablespoon of coconut milk
1/2 banana, chopped into cubes
110ml/1/2 cup of apple juice
1/2 teaspoon of fresh ginger root
2 small ice cubes or 1/2 cup crushed ice

Method

Add all ingredients to blender and process until smooth.

Banana and Crunchie Smoothie (serves 2)

Ingredients

2 bananas
2 scoops of vanilla ice-cream
110ml/1/2 cup of milk (any type)
1 Cadburys crunchie (roughly chopped)

Method

Add the milk and crunchie to blender. Blast them for 15 seconds, then add ice cream and bananas, blend for another 15 seconds.

Banana Delight Smoothie (serves 2)

Ingredients

2 bananas
1 tablespoon of Greek yoghurt
1 large teaspoon of Nutella®
1 handful of crushed ice
275ml/1/2 pint of milk

Method

Chop bananas then add them and all remaining ingredients to the blender. Blend, pour and enjoy. For the chocoholics add more Nutella® to taste.

Banana and Forest Berry Smoothie (serves 2)

Ingredients

1 medium sized banana
115g/1 cup of frozen or fresh forest fruits
225ml/1 cup of apple juice

Method

Place all ingredients into a blender and blend until smooth.

Banana Hazelnut Smoothie (serves 4)

Ingredients

4 medium bananas, peeled and sliced into 1/2 inch pieces
6 tablespoons light brown sugar
30g/1/4 cup hazelnuts
225ml/1 cup ice cubes
55ml/1/4 cup milk
2 tablespoons chopped hazelnuts, for garnish (optional)

Method

Place the sliced bananas in a sealed plastic bag and put them in the freezer for 1 hour. Place the brown sugar and the hazelnuts in a blender and grind together until fine. Place the frozen bananas, ice cubes and milk in the blender with the sugar and nut mixture. Garnish with chopped nuts, if desired.

Banana Island Smoothie (serves 2)

Ingredients

55ml/1/4 cup milk
110g/1/2 cup strawberry yoghurt
55ml/1/4 cup crushed ice
1 banana (chopped)
1/2 teaspoon honey
225ml/1 cup pineapple chunks

Method

Put all ingredients into the blend (except for the honey). Blend for approx. 20 seconds, then add the honey and whirl for a further 10 seconds.

Banana Jungle Power Smoothie (serves 2)

Ingredients

1 chopped banana
1 chopped papaya
1 chopped mango
225ml/1 cup of milk
110ml/1/2 cup of ice

Method

Blend all ingredients together and serve chilled.

Banana and Malibu Smoothie (serves 2)

Ingredients (Alcoholic)

100ml/3 1/2fl oz Malibu
2 medium bananas
1/2 tin of peaches
1 medium orange
handful of blueberries

Method

Chop the fruit up into small pieces, add to blender and blend for approx 20 seconds. Once blended add the Malibu® and blend for another 20 seconds and serve immediately.

Banana and Mango Smoothie (serves 1)

Ingredients

2 bananas

1 large mango

110ml/1/2 cup of milk

Method

Blend all ingredients together until the mixture is smooth. This recipe can be frozen and served as an ice-block for kids.

Banana Mania Smoothie (serves 1)

Ingredients

2 bananas

6 strawberries

5 raspberries

1 clementine

2 ice cubes

Method

Blend the fruits together first, then gradually add the ice.

Banana and Melon Crush Smoothie (serves 2)

Ingredients

1 banana chopped into 4

2 good slices of melon (cubed)

2 good scoops of vanilla ice cream

splash of cranberry juice

Method

Put the melon and banana into the blender, blast for 20 seconds. Next, add the splash of cranberry juice and ice cream and blend again for around 20 seconds until smooth.

Banana Milk Smoothie (serves 2)

Ingredients

2 medium bananas
570ml/1 pint of milk

Method

Chop up bananas into pieces and put in the blender for about 10 seconds, slowly add milk and blend for a further 20 seconds.

Banana and Mixed Berry Smoothie (serves 1)

Ingredients

30g/1/4 cup of fresh or frozen assorted berries
1 small banana, chopped into 4
225ml/1 cup of orange juice
4 tablespoons of low fat vanilla yoghurt

Method

Place all ingredients in the blender, blend until smooth.

Banana and Oat Smoothie (serves 1)

Ingredients

1 large or 2 small bananas
215ml/7fl oz ice cold milk
1 tablespoon rolled porridge oats
2 ice cubes

Method

Place all ingredients into the blender, mix for approximately 30 seconds.

Banana and Orange Smoothie (serves 1)

Ingredients

1 banana
225ml/1 cup of milk
225ml/1 cup of orange/pineapple juice

Method

Chop banana into 4 pieces then place all ingredients into the blender, mix for approximately 30 seconds.

Banana Peach Smoothie (serves 1)

Ingredients

1 small banana, or half a large
60g/1/2 cup unsweetened canned peaches, drained
225ml/1 cup milk
110ml/1/2 cup ice cubes

Method

Blend all ingredients together until smooth.

Banana and Peanut Butter Smoothie (serves 2)

Ingredients

1 large banana, chopped into 4
335ml/1 1/2 medium size cups of milk
2 tablespoons peanut butter
pinch of cinnamon (optional)

Method

Place all ingredients into the blender, blend until thick and smooth. Serve and enjoy.

Banana and Pineapple Smoothie (serves 2)

Ingredients

2 large ripe bananas
4 tablespoons low fat natural yoghurt
250ml/1 1/5 cup pineapple juice

Method

Cut the bananas into small pieces and put in the blender. Add the pineapple juice, then the low fat natural yoghurt. Blend until smooth.

Banana Split Smoothies (serves 2)

Ingredients

2 medium ripe bananas
1 can (225g/8 oz) crushed pineapple, drained
335ml/1 1/2 cups milk
60g/1/2 cup fresh or frozen unsweetened sliced strawberries
2 tablespoons honey
5 ice cubes
whipped topping, chocolate syrup & maraschino cherries

Method

In a blender, combine first five ingredients; cover and process until smooth. Gradually add ice, blending until slushy. Pour into chilled glasses. Garnish with whipped topping, chocolate syrup, and cherries.

Banana and Strawberry Smoothie (serves 2)

Ingredients

1 large banana
12 large strawberries
6-10 cubes of ice
sprig of mint

Method

Chop the banana into 4 pieces, then put them in the blender together with the strawberries and ice cubes. Blend until smooth. Serve in a tall glass and decorate with the mint.

Banana and Strawberry Burst Smoothie (serves 1)

Ingredients

1 large banana, chopped into 4
225ml/1 cup of milk
165g/3/4 cup of yoghurt
5 strawberries cut into halves
ice

Method

Place all ingredients into the blender, mix for approximately 30 seconds.

Banana, Strawberry and Pineapple Smoothie (serves 2)

Ingredients

12 strawberries
1 whole banana
1/2 can of pineapples (or 1 whole fresh pineapple if you prefer more)

Method

Dice strawberries (keeping just one aside), then cut banana into 4 pieces. Next use 1/2 of the can of pineapple (or whole fresh pineapple if more required), add to blender, blend till smooth. Pour smoothie in the glass and add one strawberry on top for decoration.

Banana Sweetie Smoothie (serves 2)

Ingredients

1 whole banana
30ml/1fl oz strawberry syrup
60ml/2fl oz milk
110ml/1/2 cup of cubed or crushed ice

Method

Place the banana in blender, then add the ice, syrup then the milk.

Banana Toffee Smoothie (serves 2)

Ingredients

2 large bananas, quartered
1 low fat toffee yoghurt
1 medium sized cup of milk

Method

Add the bananas to the blender, next add the yoghurt then the milk, mix for approximately 20 seconds. Serve and enjoy!

Banana Tropical Smoothie (serves 2)

Ingredients

2 bananas
1 mango
2 kiwis
1/2 a papaya
10-12 frozen strawberries
225-450ml/1-2 cups cranberry juice

Method

Add all ingredients to blender and process until smooth.

Banana & Vanilla Smoothie (serves 2)

Ingredients

2 chopped bananas
150ml/2/3 cup of milk
2 scoops of vanilla ice cream
2 ice cubes
crushed vanilla pod or vanilla extract (optional)

Method

Add all ingredients to blender and process until smooth.

Banana Vanilla-Iced Vodka Smoothie (serves 2)

Ingredients - (Alcoholic)

2 bananas
2 small scoops vanilla ice cream
1 medium cup of milk
100ml/3 1/2fl oz vodka

Method

Chop the fruit, place in the blender and add ice cream, mix and add milk (a little at a time). Stop and add vodka, mix for a further 10 seconds.

Create your own banana smoothie recipes and write them here:-

Name

Ingredients

Method

Name

Ingredients

Method

Name

Ingredients

Method

Berry Berry Smoothie (serves 2)

Ingredients

2 kiwis, peeled and cut into 4 pieces
1 banana
5 strawberries
7 raspberries
335g/1 1/2 cup low fat natural yoghurt
1 medium size glass milk

Method

Put all ingredients in the blender, blend until desired consistency, serve immediately. If you think it is too thick, just add more milk.

Berry Bonanza Smoothie (serves 2)

Ingredients

20 blueberries
20 strawberries
2 mangos
25ml/3 teaspoons pure apple juice

Method

Cut the mangos up into small pieces then add to blender. Next add the apple juice, blueberries and strawberries. Blend until smooth. For a more creamier and colder version, try adding a little bit of vanilla ice cream to the mix.

Berry Burst Smoothie (serves 2)

Ingredients

1 handful of raspberries
1 chopped mango
1 lime (juice only)
2 peeled oranges
splash of apple juice
6 ice cubes

Method

Blend together your mango, oranges and raspberries. Then add your lime juice and splash of apple juice, blend again. Finally add your ice, blend until cubes are crushed.

Berry Delight Smoothie (serves 2)

Ingredients

150ml/2/3 cup raspberry yoghurt
75ml/1/3 cup natural yoghurt
50ml/3 tablespoons milk
50g/1/2 cup frozen raspberries
2 pears peeled, cored and chopped

Method

Blend all ingredients for 30 seconds until smooth, keeping a little of the natural yoghurt aside to dribble on top of your finished smoothie.

Berry Fruity Smoothie (serves 2)

Ingredients

25g/1/4 cup raspberries
75ml/1/3 cup of non-fat, sugar free vanilla yoghurt
225ml/1 cup of orange juice
1 small banana, chop into 4 pieces

Method

Chop the banana into 4 pieces, then place all ingredients in the blender and blend until smooth.

Berry Refresher (serves 2)

Ingredients

2 bananas
115g/1 cup of raspberries
60g/1/2 cup frozen blueberries
10-12 frozen strawberries
225-450ml/1-2 cups cranberry juice

Method

Place all ingredients in a blender and blend until smooth.

Berry-Tastic Smoothie (serves 1)

Ingredients

1 handful of blueberries
3 plums
1/2 glass of cranberry juice
4 tablespoons of Greek yoghurt
1 banana
4-5 ice cubes

Method

Remove the stone from the plums and roughly chop them and place in the blender. Add the blueberries, banana, cranberry juice, greek yoghurt, then the ice.

Berry Tropical Fruit Smoothie (serves 4)

Ingredients

2 apples
6 large strawberries
1 large cup of berries
1 large cup of chopped/cubed pineapple
1 medium cup of ice (cubed or crushed)
1 medium cup of fresh orange juice
1 pot of natural yoghurt

Method

Put everything in the blender and blast on highest speed. The ice makes it cold and the yoghurt adds flavour and makes it creamy.

Berry and Peach Smoothie (serves 2)

Ingredients

60g/1/2 cup ripe medium peaches, diced
60g/1/2 cup raspberries
150ml/3/4 cup peach nectar
225g/1 cup low-fat peach yoghurt

Method

Combine the yoghurt and nectar in a blender. Add the raspberries and peaches. Blend until smooth.

Berry and Mango Blast Smoothie (serves 4)

Ingredients (Alcoholic)

1 whole mango

1/2 punnet of strawberries

1/2 punnet of raspberries

1 large cup of ice cubes

2 shots of vodka

Method

Blend altogether until ice nearly gone.

Berry and Vodka Smoothie (serves 1)

Ingredients (Alcoholic)

cherries

6 strawberries

6 raspberries

110ml/1/2 cup lemon lime soda

1 peach

12 grapes

1 banana

100ml/3 1/2fl oz vodka

Method

Roughly chop the fruit, add to blender. Pour in the lemon lime soda and vodka (add ice if preferred). Blend.

Blackberry, Cherry and Apple Pie Smoothie (serves 2)

Ingredients

approx 20 cherries

1 apple

1 banana

1 kiwi

1 handful of blueberries

cloudy apple juice

Method

Stone the cherries and put into the blender. Add the chopped apple, banana, kiwi and blueberries. Blend with a splash of apple juice to loosen.

Blackberry Ice Cream Smoothie (serves 2)

Ingredients

60g/1/2 cup blackberries (fresh or frozen)
110ml/1/2 cup vanilla ice cream
1/2 banana
110ml/1/2 cup milk

Method

Blend the milk with the banana and and blackberries until a slushy texture is formed. Add ice cream for extra sweetness and blend till smooth.

Blackberry and Cherry Smoothie (serves 2)

Ingredients

115g/1 cup cherries
60g/1/2 cup of blackberries
1 large glass of water

Method

Place ingredients in the blender and blend until smooth.

Blackberry and Honeydew Melon Smoothie (serves 2)

Ingredients

230g/2 cups of frozen blackberries
230g/2 cups honeydew melon (fresh or frozen)
40g/1/3 cup of sugar (or more to taste)

Method

Puree all ingredients in a blender. Blend. Pour and serve.

Blissful Berries Smoothie (serves 2)

Ingredients

115g/1 medium cup of raspberries
115g/1 medium cup of strawberries
1 banana
450ml/2 cups of orange juice

Method

Put all the fruit and juice into the blender, then blend until smooth.

Blueberry Blast Smoothie (serves 2)

Ingredients

110ml/1/2 cup of skimmed milk
225g/1 cup of low fat vanilla ice cream
230g/2 cups of frozen blueberries

Method

Put all ingredients in the blender and blend until smooth.

Blueberry and Blackcurrant Burst Smoothie (serves 2)

Ingredients

250g/2 cups fresh blackcurrants
125g/1 cup blueberries
6 ice cubes
1 teaspoon of honey or sugar (optional)

Method

Place all ingredients in a blender. Blend. Pour and serve.

Blueberry and Pineapple Smoothie (serves 2)

Ingredients

230g/2 cups of chilled fresh or frozen blueberries, slightly thawed
225ml/1 cup of chilled pineapple or orange juice
225g/8oz carton of low-fat vanilla yoghurt
1 tablespoon of sugar

Method

In a blender, combine all ingredients. Cover and blend for between 1-2 minutes until nearly smooth.

Blueberry and Yoghurt Smoothie (serves 1)

Ingredients

60g/1/2 cup of wild blueberries
110g/1/2 cup of blueberry yoghurt
1/2 a banana
3 cubes of ice

Method

Blend the banana, ice and yoghurt together until the banana is well blended. Add the blueberries and blend on low speed for 30 seconds. Adding the blueberries at the end leaves the blueberry flavour at the top.

Cinnamon Surprise Smoothie (serves 2)

Ingredients

2 bananas
1 small cup of frozen raspberries
1 small cup of frozen blueberries
1 small cup of pure orange juice
1 teaspoon vanilla essence
1 teaspoon maple syrup
3 ice cubes
cinnamon to taste

Method

Place all ingredients in the blender and blend until smooth. The more cinnamon added the more delicious it is.

Cranberry Smoothie (serves 1)

Ingredients

225g/1 cup cranberry juice, chilled
6 medium strawberries, hulls removed and cut into halves
1/2 banana, cut into quarters
110ml/1/2 cup crushed ice

Method

Put all ingredients in a blender. Blend for a few seconds on high speed or until ingredients are thoroughly combined.

Cranberry and Orange Squeeze Smoothie (serves 2)

Ingredients

225ml/1 cup cranberry juice
110ml/1/2 cup sorbet, raspberry flavour
1 tablespoon orange juice concentrate
60g/1/2 cup of orange segments
60g/1/2 cup fresh cranberries, or cherries (if preferred)

Method

Combine the cranberry juice, sorbet, and orange juice concentrate in a blender. Add the orange sections and cranberries. Blend until smooth.

Cranberry and Strawberry Smoothie (serves 2)

Ingredients

225ml/8fl oz cranberry juice
5 strawberries cut into halves
5 ice cubes

Method

Place all ingredients into blender, and process until smooth.

Mixed Berry Madness Smoothie (serves 2)

Ingredients

1/2 cup of frozen mixed berries
1/2 ltr/2 1/4 cups apple juice
2 tablespoons of honey
1 tablespoon of natural yoghurt

Method

Add mixed berries to blender, then add apple juice, honey and yoghurt. Blend until smooth. Serve and enjoy.

Raspberry Margarita Smoothie (serves 2)

Ingredients (Alcoholic)

15-20 raspberries
2 cups of crushed ice
150ml/2/3 cup margarita mixer
2 shots tequilla
1 tablespoon orange juice concentrate
2 teaspoons sweetened lime juice

Method

Put raspberries in a blender, then add margarita mixer, tequilla, orange juice concentrate and sweetened lime juice, add crushed ice on top. Blend until nearly smooth. Pour into 2 glasses and garnish with whole raspberries.

Raspberry Protein Smoothie (serves 2)

Ingredients

60g/1/2 cup frozen unsweetened raspberries
40g/1/3 cup oats
1 tablespoon fat-free vanilla yoghurt
110ml/1/2 cup skimmed milk
2 tablespoons vanilla or chocolate powder (optional)

Method

Firstly blend ice, milk and yoghurt together. Next add the powder (optional) and oats, blend again. Then add raspberries and pulse several times to make sure it is mixed well.

Raspberry Ripple Smoothie (serves 2)

Ingredients

1 medium banana
60g/1/2 cup of red raspberries (or strawberries)
60g/1/2 cup of blackberries (or blueberries)
110g/1/2 cup of yoghurt
110ml/1/2 cup of ice

Method

Cut the raspberries into small pieces that will fit through a straw. Blend the banana, ice, and yoghurt with the blackberries. Layer alternating chopped raspberries and smoothies through the glass.

Raspberry and Lemon Smoothie (serves 1)

Ingredients

15 raspberries
lemonade - a good splash (should not cover the raspberries)

Method

Place raspberries in the blender, pour over some lemonade (making sure you don't cover them). Blend for approximately 20 seconds, serve and enjoy.

Raspberry and Orange Tang Smoothie (serves 2)

Ingredients

10 raspberries
juice squeezed from 5 oranges
50ml/1 2/3fl oz still water
50ml/1 2/3fl oz cranberry juice

Method

Place raspberries in the blender first, then add the freshly squeezed orange juice. Blend for 10-15 seconds. Add cranberry juice and water. Mix on high for 8 more seconds.

Tip: This smoothie has more of a juice consistency than being a thick smoothie consistency, so if you prefer it to be thicker just add less or no water.

Raspberry and Peach Soft Smoothie (serves 2)

Ingredients

275g/10oz frozen raspberries (slightly thawed)
225ml/1 cup peach juice
110ml/1/2 cup buttermilk
1 tablespoon of honey

Method

Place all ingredients into blender, and process until smooth.

Summer Berry Smoothie (serves 2)

Ingredients

350g/3 cups of summer fruits (frozen)
1 banana
1 glass of pure apple juice

Method

Blend all ingredients in blender till smooth. Sieve seeds out if not blended. Serve and enjoy.

Triple Berry Smoothie (serves 2)

Ingredients

60g/1/2 cup blueberries
60g/1/2 cup raspberries
1 banana
110g/1/2 cup yoghurt
225ml/1 cup milk
110ml/1/2 cup ice cubes

Method

Blend the banana, ice, yoghurt, milk, and other berries together until a smooth drink is formed. Pour into a cup and enjoy a very fruity, healthy smoothie.

Very Berry Smoothie (serves 2)

Ingredients

30g/1/4 cup of blueberries
30g/1/4 cup of raspberries
1 large banana
100ml/3 1/2fl oz of low fat berry yoghurt, orange juice and ice

Method

Place all ingredients in mixer. Blend for approximately 30 seconds.

Create your own berry smoothie recipes and write them here:-

Name

Ingredients

Method

Name

Ingredients

Method

Name

Ingredients

Method

Simply Strawberries Smoothie (serves 2)

Ingredients

12 strawberries
165g/3/4 cup of strawberry yoghurt
1 scoop of strawberry ice cream

Method

Chop the strawberries (keeping aside a few pieces for garnish) and blend with yoghurt and ice cream. Serve and garnish with strawberry pieces.

Strawberry Cherry Berry Smoothie (serves 4)

Ingredients

345g/3 cups frozen pitted dark sweet cherries
345g/3 cups frozen whole strawberries
675ml/3 cups cranberry juice

Method

In a blender, puree half the frozen pitted dark sweet cherries, half the frozen strawberries and half the cranberry juice, stirring as needed, until smooth. Pour into two serving glasses. Repeat with remaining ingredients for two more servings.

Strawberry De-Lish Smoothie (serves 1)

Ingredients

1 large ripe mango
half a punnet of strawberries
1 banana

Method

Place all ingredients into a blender and mix with ice.

Strawberry Fizz Smoothie (serves 2)

Ingredients

250g/2 1/4 cup strawberries
2 apples, cored and chopped into large cubes
300ml/1 1/3 cup orange juice

Method

Put all ingredients into the blender, and blend until desired consistency.

Strawberry Ice Smoothie (serves 2)

Ingredients (Alcoholic)

8 strawberries

8 ice cubes

1/3 glass of vodka

1 freshly squeezed lemon

Method

Blend the strawberries and ice cubes. Next add your vodka and lemon juice, mix together until smooth. Pour into a glass and enjoy!

Strawberry Fruit Burst Smoothie (serves 1)

Ingredients

2 bananas

1 orange

2 kiwis

10-12 frozen strawberries

60g/1/2 cup of frozen blueberries

225-450ml/1-2 cups of orange juice

Method

Blend all ingredients together and serve chilled.

Strawberry, Mango and Orange Smoothie (serves 2)

Ingredients

2 handfuls of strawberries (sliced and hulled)

1 large mango (sliced)

335ml/1 1/2 medium size cups of pure orange juice

4 ice cubes

Method

Place all ingredients into a blender, blend until there are no lumps. Put mixture in the fridge for 5-10 minutes, then serve, drink immediately and enjoy.

Strawberry Mania Smoothie (serves 1)

Ingredients

6 strawberries
1 banana
5 raspberries
1 clementine
2 ice-cubes

Method

Blend the fruits together first, then gradually add the ice.

Strawberry Margarita Smoothie (serves 2)

Ingredients (Alcoholic)

15 strawberries
2 cups of crushed ice
2/3 cup margarita mixer
2 shots tequilla
1 tablespoon orange juice concentrate
2 teaspoons sweetened lime juice

Method

Put strawberries in a blender, then add margarita mixer, tequilla, orange juice concentrate and sweetened lime juice, add crushed ice on top. Blend until nearly smooth. Pour into 2 glasses and garnish with whole strawberries.

Strawberry Multi-Fruit Yoghurt Smoothie (serves 1)

Ingredients

half ripe mango
6 fresh/frozen strawberries
1 banana
1 small apple
5 tablespoons strawberry yoghurt
5 ice cubes

Method

Peel and chunk all the fruit and put in blender, add yoghurt then ice cubes. Blend for approx 40 seconds till smooth.

Strawberry, Orange and Kiwi Smoothie (serves 2)

Ingredients

250g/9oz fresh strawberries
300ml/1 1/3 cups pure orange juice
2 kiwi fruit, peeled and core removed
1 teaspoon of honey (optional)
1 halved strawberry and 2 slices of peeled kiwi fruit to decorate the glass

Method

Blend all ingredients until smooth. Decorate the glasses, then serve.

Strawberry Orange Splash Smoothie (serves 2)

Ingredients

10 strawberries (save 2 for garnish)
1 medium sized cup of fresh orange juice
1/4 orange
6 ice cubes

Method

Chop 8 strawberries in halves. Peel and slice the 1/4 of orange, put all the ingredients in a blender and mix until smooth. Pour into 2 glasses and garnish with a strawberry in each.

Strawberry Smoothie (serves 2)

Ingredients

1 cup or 6 large fresh strawberries
225ml/1 cup milk
110g/1/2 cup vanilla yoghurt
4 ice cubes

Method

Put all the ingredients in blender and blend until smooth. Pour into glasses and serve immediately.

Strawberry Shot Smoothie (serves 2)

Ingredients

170ml/6fl oz orange juice
60ml/2fl oz milk
1 peeled and frozen banana
3 to 5 frozen strawberries
1 fresh peeled peach
1/2 teaspoon cinnamon

Method

Put all ingredients in a blender and whip at high speed until smooth. Pour into two glasses.

Strawberry Slushy Smoothie (serves 1)

Ingredients

4 large strawberries
1 teaspoon of sugar
110ml/1/2 cup of whole milk
225ml/1 cup of ice cubes

Method

Blend strawberries with milk on low speed till smooth, then add ice cubes and blend on high. Add sugar and blend on high speed for about 1 minute. The texture should be slushy and smooth.

Strawberry Smooth Smoothie (serves 1)

Ingredients

2 bananas
10-12 frozen strawberries
225ml/1 cup of apple juice

Method

Blend all ingredients together and serve chilled.

Strawberry Summer Sun Smoothie (serves 2)

Ingredients

2 kiwis
half a punnet of strawberries
2 apples
1 large orange

Method

Chop each piece of fruit up into reasonably small pieces then put all into the blender. Blend until your desired consistency. Serve.

Strawberry Sweetie Smoothie (serves 2)

Ingredients

6 large strawberries
30ml/1fl oz strawberry syrup
60ml/2fl oz milk
110ml/1/2 cup of cubed or crushed ice

Method

Place the strawberries in blender, then add the ice, syrup then the milk.

Strawberry and Apple Smoothie (serves 1)

Ingredients

150g/1 1/3 cup strawberries
1 apple

Method

Cut up the strawberries and the apple and put them in the blender. Blend until desired consistency, then pour into a glass with a strawberry on a cocktail stick for decoration.

Strawberry and Apple Blast Smoothie (serves 2)

Ingredients

2 bananas
1 green apple
1 red apple
10-12 frozen strawberries
225-450ml/1-2 cups apple juice

Method

Blend all ingredients until smooth. Decorate the glasses, then serve.

Strawberry and Banana Smoothie (serves 1)

Ingredients

1 small banana
6 large strawberries
5 cubes of ice

Method

Chop the banana into 4 pieces, then put them in the blender together with the strawberries and ice cubes. Blend until smooth. Serve in a tall glass.

Strawberry and Banana Burst Smoothie (serves 1)

Ingredients

1 large banana, chopped into 4
225ml/1 cup of milk
200g/7oz of strawberry yoghurt
5 strawberries cut into halves
ice

Method

Place all ingredients into the blender, mix for approximately 30 seconds.

Strawberry and Banana Smoothie (serves 2)

Ingredients

1 large banana
12 large strawberries
6-10 cubes of ice
Sprig of mint

Method

Chop the banana into 4 pieces, then put them in the blender together with the strawberries and ice cubes. Blend until smooth. Serve in a tall glass and decorate with the mint.

Strawberry and Banana Yoghurt Smoothie (serves 2)

Ingredients

165ml/3/4 cup apple juice
110g/1/2 cup natural yoghurt
1 banana, sliced and frozen
115g/1 cup frozen strawberries

Method

Pour the apple juice into a blender. Add the yoghurt and process until smooth. Add the frozen banana slices and half of the strawberries and process well, then add the remaining strawberries and process until smooth.

Strawberry and Cranberry Smoothie (serves 2)

Ingredients

225ml/8fl oz cranberry juice
5 strawberries cut into halves
5 ice cubes

Method

Place all ingredients into blender, and process until smooth.

Strawberries and Cream Smoothie (serve 2)

Ingredients

12 large strawberries
2 scoops of vanilla ice cream
1 cup of ice
1 drop of vanilla essence
strawberry sauce (optional)

Method

Blend the strawberries, ice cream, ice and vanilla essence until required consistency. Pour into a glass and decorate top of smoothie with strawberry sauce.

Strawberry and Kiwi Smoothie (serves 2)

Ingredients

12 strawberries
2 kiwis
1 banana
1 tablespoon of honey
4 large ice cubes

Method

Slice the bananas into four. Cut tops the off the strawberries, peel and dice the kiwis then add all to blender. Add 1 tablespoon of honey then 4 ice cubes and blend for approx 20 seconds.

Strawberry and Lemon Smoothie (serves 2)

Ingredients

350ml/1 1/2 cups lemonade
165g/3/4 cup strawberry yoghurt
4 strawberries
3 ice cubes

Method

Place all ingredients into smoothie maker, mix for 10 seconds, then smooth for 10 seconds.

Strawberry and Lemon Yoghurt Smoothie (serves 1)

Ingredients

1/2 teaspoon lemon zest
1 teaspoon of lemon juice
60g/1/2 cup strawberries
110ml/1/2 cup orange juice
225g/1 cup of low-fat vanilla yoghurt
1/2 cup of crushed ice (or 4 ice cubes)

Method

Place all ingredients in the blender. Blend for approximately 30 seconds, serve.

Strawberry and Peach Delight Smoothie (serves 4)

Ingredients

1 punnet of strawberries
1 medium-sized tin of peaches
1-2 pots of strawberry and peach yoghurt

Method

Cut up the strawberries and add to blender. Next add the tin of peaches (juice included). Then add in 1 or two pots of strawberry and peach yoghurt (this can be replaced with natural yoghurt if preferred) place in a blender and blend till smooth.

Strawberry and Pineapple Smoothie (serves 2)

Ingredients

12 strawberries
1 scoop of vanilla ice cream
1/2 can of pineapples (or 1 whole fresh pineapple if you prefer more)

Method

Dice strawberries (keeping just one aside). Next use the can of pineapple (or whole fresh pineapple if more required) and add to blender with the ice cream and blend till smooth. Pour smoothie in the glass and add one strawberry on top for decoration.

Strawberry and Raspberry Smoothie (serves 2)

Ingredients

230g/2 cups of frozen strawberries and raspberries
75ml/1/3 cup of milk
2 teaspoons of honey
2 scoops of vanilla ice cream
175g/6 oz of yoghurt

Method

Place everything in the blender. Blend for approximately 20 seconds, serve and enjoy.

Strawberry and Watermelon Smoothie (serves 2)

Ingredients

150g/1 1/5 cup strawberries
1/8 of a watermelon

Method

Put watermelon and strawberries into the blender (keeping two strawberries aside for decoration), blend for approximately 20 seconds. Pour into two glasses and garnish each glass with a strawberry on a cocktail stick.

Summer Smoothie (serves 2)

Ingredients

150g/1 1/5 cup strawberries (tops off)
10g/1/4 oz raspberries
2 chopped and peeled apples
2 bananas
1 small cup of pineapple juice
55g/1/3 cup natural yoghurt
1 small cup of crushed ice

Method

Add the strawberries and raspberries to the blender, next add the pineapple juice, apples, bananas, yoghurt then the ice. Mix for 30-40 seconds.

Summer Red Smoothie (serves 2)

Ingredients

8 large strawberries
1/2 banana
1 orange
3 pineapple slices
1 medium cup of pure apple juice
1 medium cup of crushed ice

Method

Put all ingredients (except ice) in blender and blend for approx. 30 seconds. Next add the ice and blend until your preferred texture. Serve immediately for best results. Perfect for hot Summer days!

Sweet, Sweet Strawberry Smoothie (serves 2)

Ingredients

10 chopped (cooled) strawberries
5 ice cubes
40ml/1 1/2fl oz semi-skimmed milk
1/2 teaspoons of vanilla essence
4 teaspoons of icing sugar

Method

Put the strawberries, ice cubes and milk into the blender and blend until smooth. Next, add the vanilla essence and icing sugar and blend them in. Serve.

Thick Strawberry Smoothie (serves 2)

Ingredients

6 large strawberries
110g/1/2 cup of your favourite yoghurt
110ml/1/2 cup of vanilla or strawberry ice cream
110ml/1/2 cup of whole milk

Method

First blend strawberries and milk together until strawberries are well blended, then add ice cream and yoghurt and whip for just a little bit so smoothie remains thick.

Tropical Strawberry Smoothie (serves 1)

Ingredients

1 banana

1 orange

2 chunks of fresh pineapple

6 frozen strawberries

225ml/1 cup of orange juice

Method

Blend all ingredients together and serve chilled.

Tropical Strawberry and Malibu® Smoothie (serves 2)

Ingredients (Alcoholic)

2 bananas

2 oranges

3 chunks of fresh pineapple

10-12 frozen strawberries

225ml/1 cup of orange juice

55ml/1/4 cup of Malibu®

Method

Blend all ingredients together and serve chilled.

Very Very Strawberry Smoothie (serves 1)

Ingredients

12 strawberries

1 teaspoon of strawberry syrup

1 scoop of strawberry ice cream

1 teaspoon of single cream

Method

Chop the strawberries (keeping aside a few pieces for garnish) and blend with ice cream and syrup. Serve and garnish with strawberry pieces.

Create your own strawberry smoothie recipes and write them here:-

Name

Ingredients

Method

Name

Ingredients

Method

Name

Ingredients

Method

Apricot Pineapple Smoothie (serves 1)

Ingredients

30g/1/4 cup crushed pineapple
1 fresh apricot, diced
6 strawberries
1/2 banana
335ml/1 1/2 cup water
1 tablespoon skim milk powder

Method

In a blender, process fruit with the rest of the ingredients. Blend until thoroughly mixed and serve.

Apricot, Honey and Orange Smoothie (serves 2)

Ingredients

150g/5oz dried apricots
1 orange, juice only
60ml/2fl oz milk
1 tablespoon honey
90ml/3fl oz ice

Method

Roughly chop the apricots, then add all the ingredients to blender and process until smooth.

Chocolate Orange Dream Smoothie (serves 2)

Ingredients

8 squares of milk chocolate
1 medium/large orange
5 strawberries
1 good scoop of chocolate ice cream

Method

Break up the chocolate and chop the fruit into small pieces, place them in the blender. Next add the ice cream and blend/whiz until smooth.

Coconut and Apple Smoothie (serves 1)

Ingredients

55ml/1/4 cup apple juice
1 tablespoon coconut milk
1/2 banana
1/4 teaspoon grated fresh ginger root
1/2 cup crushed ice, or 2 small ice cubes

Method

Add all ingredients to blender and process until smooth.

Cool Peach and Clementine Smoothie (serves 2)

Ingredients

2 frozen peaches, cubed
3 clementines (or satsumas)
75ml/1/3 cup orange juice
55ml/1/4 cup lemonade (or more orange juice if preferred)
4 ice cubes

Method

Put all ingredients into blender (liquids and fruit first, then frozen fruit and ice). Blend until smooth, serve and enjoy!

Kiwi Tang Smoothie (serves 2)

Ingredients

60g/1/2 cup of fresh diced kiwi
60g/1/2 cup of lime sherbet
115g/1 cup of diced ripe banana
115g/1 cup of diced honeydew melon

Method

Put all ingredients in the blender then blend until smooth.

Energy Blast Smoothie (serves 2)

Ingredients

340ml/12fl oz of milk
1 egg
225g/1 cup of flavoured yoghurt
1 piece of fruit (banana, kiwi, orange, etc.)

Method

Mix all ingredients into a blender, add some ice for chill, and presto!

Fruit Crush Smoothie (serves 2)

Ingredients

110ml/1/2 medium sized cup of cloudy lemonade
110g/1/2 cup of low fat natural yoghurt
1 handful frozen forest fruits
1 handful of frozen tropical fruit

Method

Put liquid ingredients into the blender first, then add the fruit and blend for approximately 40 seconds.

Frothy Tropical Smoothie (serves 3)

Ingredients

1 1/2 medium size cups of chopped pineapple
1 1/2 medium size cups of chopped mango
1 banana, peeled and chopped
500ml/17 1/2fl oz smooth orange juice
1 scoop vanilla ice cream
2 tablespoon honey

Method

Put banana, mango and pineapple in the blender. Next add juice and honey followed by the ice cream. Blend for a total of 1 minute.

Fruity-Galore Smoothie (serves 1)

Ingredients

2 slices of pineapple
20ml/4 teaspoons of pineapple juice
1 small cup of red grapes
1 small cup of white grapes
2 ice cubes

Method

Put everything into a blender, mix for 20 seconds. Pour and enjoy.

Fusion Blast Smoothie (serves 3-4)

Ingredients

1 mango
2 guavas
300ml/1 1/3 cup passion fruit juice
2 handfuls of crushed ice

Method

Chop guava into chunks, then cut mango flesh away from stone. Next add all the ingredients to your smoothie maker and hit smooth until desired consistency.

Grapes Galore Smoothie (serves 2)

Ingredients

230g/2 cups of green seedless grapes
230g/2 cups of red seedless grapes
110ml/1/2 cup purple grape juice
2 teaspoons of lime juice
1 teaspoon of peeled and minced fresh ginger root
3 ice cubes

Method

Put all ingredients in the blender and blend until smooth.

Green Fruit Smoothie (serves 2)

Ingredients

2 peeled kiwi fruits
approx 25 frozen green grapes, halved
1 frozen green apple, sliced
4-5 ice cubes
orange/apple juice to smooth it out

Method

Put all ingredients in blender including some juice. Blend. Add more juice if necessary.

Guava, Passionfruit and Mango (serves 1)

Ingredients

1 mango
2 guavas
300ml/1 1/3 cup passion fruit juice
2 handfuls of ice

Method

Chop guava into chunks, cut mango flesh away from stone and blend with juice and ice until smooth.

The High-C Smoothie (serves 2)

Ingredients

2 bananas
1 orange
2 kiwis
10-12 frozen strawberries
60g/1/2 cup of frozen blueberries
225-450ml/1-2 cups of orange juice

Method

Blend all ingredients together until smooth.

Jamaican Ginger Smoothie (serves 1)

Ingredients

1 banana chopped
fresh ginger (optional)
4-5 large strawberries
225ml/1 cup of cranberry juice
225-450ml/1 1/2 - 2 cups of ice

Method

Put everything into blender. Blend at high speed until ice is smooth. For an added touch, garnish with mint leaves.

Juicy Joe's Smoothie (serves 6)

Ingredients

about 24 juicy clementines, plus an extra one for decoration
2 small, very ripe and juicy mangoes
2 ripe bananas
500g low-fat yoghurt
handful of ice cubes (optional)

Method

Halve clementines and squeeze out the juice. Peel mangoes, then chop the flesh into rough pieces. Peel and slice the bananas then blend the clementine juice, mango flesh, bananas, yoghurt and ice cubes into a blender and blend until smooth.

Kiwi Dream Smoothie (serves 1)

Ingredients

150ml/2/3 cup milk
juice of 2 limes
2 kiwi fruit, peeled and chopped
1 tablespoon sugar
450ml/2 cups vanilla ice cream

Method

Add the milk, lime juice, sugar and ice cream and blend until mixed and smooth. Then add the kiwi fruit and process until smooth.

Lemon and Melon Burst Smoothie (serves 2)

Ingredients

60g/1/2 cup of diced honeydew melon
110g/1/2 cup of low fat lemon yoghurt
115g/1 cup frozen green grapes
1 tablespoon of chopped fresh mint
fresh lemon juice to taste (if preferred)

Method

Put the honeydew melon and lemon yoghurt in a blender. Next add the grapes and mint then blend until smooth. Taste and add lemon juice if you like.

Mango and Ginger Smoothie (serves 2)

Ingredients

225g/8oz low fat vanilla yoghurt
225ml/1 cup of non-fat buttermilk
2 pieces of crystallized ginger (approx. 1 oz)
2 ripe mangos, peeled and chopped into small pieces
110ml/1/2 cup of crushed ice

Method

In the blender purée the fruit and ginger, scraping down the sides as necessary. Add the buttermilk, yoghurt and ice and purée until smooth and frothy. Add crushed ice. Serve.

Mango Lassi Smoothie (serves 4)

Ingredients

2 mangos
2 tablespoons of Greek yoghurt
55ml/1/4 pint of milk
225ml/1 cup of ice

Method

Blend the mangos, yoghurt, milk and ice together. Add sugar if you wish.

Mango Madness Smoothie (serves 2)

Ingredients

450g/2 cups of low-fat vanilla yoghurt
225ml/1 cup mango nectar
2 mangos, peeled and chopped
1/4 teaspoon of cardamom

Method

Place all ingredients into blender, and process until smooth.

Mango Pineapple Breeze Smoothie (serves 2)

Ingredients

340ml/12fl oz can of frozen orange juice concentrate
170ml/6fl oz of mango premium nectar
225ml/1 cup of pineapple juice
225ml/1 cup of ice cubes

Method

Blend in smoothie machine or covered blender until nice and smooth. Approx 20 seconds.

Mango Squeeze Smoothie (serves 2)

Ingredients

2 grapefruits
1 mango
6 ice cubes

Method

Place all ingredients into blender, and process for approximately 1 minute or until smooth.

Melon Medley Smoothie (serves 1)

Ingredients

225g/1 cup natural yoghurt
90g/3/4 cup honeydew melon, roughly chopped
90g/3/4 cup watermelon, roughly chopped
90g/3/4 cup canteloupe melon, roughly chopped
6 ice cubes

Method

Pour the yoghurt into the blender. Add the honeydew pieces and process until smooth. Then add the cantaloupe and watermelon pieces along with the ice cubes.

Morning Burst Smoothie (serves 1)

Ingredients

1 orange
1 banana
1 apple (peeled and cored)
2-3 tablespoons orange juice concentrate
ice cubes and water for texture

Method

Cut all fruit into small chunks, place in blender. Next add water and orange juice concentrate, then blend for approx 20-30 seconds adding ice for texture as desired.

Orange Aniseed Twist Smoothie (serves 2)

Ingredients

3 oranges
2 sticks of celery (each chopped into 4 pieces)
1/4 fennel bulb

Method

Place all ingredients into blender, and mix for approximately 30 seconds in total. Serve.

Orange Delight Smoothie (serves 4)

Ingredients

180ml/6fl oz can frozen orange juice concentrate
225ml/1 cup of water
225ml/1 cup of skimmed milk
1 teaspoon of vanilla extract
10 ice cubes

Method

Place all ingredients into blender, and process until smooth.

Orange Fruity Smoothie (serves 2)

Ingredients

1 banana, chopped and cut into 4
1 peach, halved, pitted and cut into cubes
1 cup raspberries
110ml/1/2 cup freshly squeezed orange juice
3 ice cubes

Method

Place all ingredients into blender, and process until smooth.

Orange Mango Smoothie (serves 2)

Ingredients

175g/1 1/2 small cups of chopped mango
450ml/2 cups of fresh orange juice
2 tablespoons of sugar

Method

Blend all the ingredients in the blender and blend until desired consistency.

Papaya and Raspberry Smoothie (serves 1)

Ingredients

1 frozen banana, peeled
1/2 fresh papaya
10-12 raspberries (fresh or frozen)
300ml/1 1/3 cup fruit juice

Method

Pour all ingredients into smoothie maker, then whiz until smoothie consistency is reached.

Papaya, Honey and Cinnamon (serves 1)

Ingredients

1 large papaya
2 tablespoons honey
cinnamon to taste
200ml/4/5 cup greek style yoghurt
handful of ice

Method

De-stone and de-skin papaya, chop into chunks and blend all ingredients until smooth.

Passion Fruit and Banana Smoothie (serves 2)

Ingredients

1 large banana
2 passion fruits
450ml/2 cups milk
2 drops vanilla essence
3-4 ice cubes (optional)

Method

Slice the banana, halve the passion fruits and scoop out the seeds and fruit and add to the blender. Add the milk, vanilla essence and ice cubes if adding, and blend on high until all the ingredients are well blended.

Passion Fruit, Mango & Pineapple Smoothie (serves 1)

Ingredients

2 passion fruits, pulp only
1 small mango, cut into chunks
75g of pineapple, cut into chunks
75ml of pineapple juice
1 lime, juice only
7 ice cubes
a pinch of ground black pepper
a pinch of cayenne pepper (optional)

Method

Blend all of the ingredients together until smooth. If you prefer your smoothie to have a little "kick" add a pinch of cayenne pepper.

Passion Fruit and Strawberry Chill (serves 2)

Ingredients

handful of frozen strawberries
1 banana
150ml/2/3 cup yoghurt (mango, papaya and passionfruit is best)
200ml/4/5 cup passion fruit juice

Method

Mix in the smoothie maker until smooth.

Peachy Banana Smoothie (serves 2)

Ingredients

1 medium sized tin of peaches
1 large banana
1 small cup of fresh orange juice

Method

Break up the banana and put in your blender. Next add the tin of peaches (drained of syrup). Then add enough orange juice to cover your banana pieces, blend until desired consistency, then serve and enjoy.

Peach and Orange Smoothie (serves 2)

Ingredients

1/2 tin of peaches
2 tablespoons of natural yoghurt
250-400ml/1-2 cups of fresh orange juice

Method

Open the tin of peaches and put half of the peaches into the blender (pour approx two thirds of the syrup in also). Next, add the natural yoghurt. Finally add between 250-400ml/1-2 cups of the orange juice depending on preference. Blend well, serve and enjoy.

Pineapple and Banana Smoothie (serves 2)

Ingredients

2 large ripe bananas
4 tablespoons low fat natural yoghurt
225ml/1 cup pineapple juice

Method

Cut the bananas into small pieces and put in the blender. Add the pineapple juice, then the low fat natural yoghurt. Blend until smooth.

Pineapple and Cherry Vanilla Smoothie (serves 2)

Ingredients

1/2 teaspoon of vanilla extract
225ml/1 cup of pineapple juice
230g/2 cups of unsweetened frozen cherries
230g/2 cups of frozen raspberries
450g/2 cups of frozen low-fat vanilla yoghurt
450ml/2 cups of ice

Method

Put all ingredients in the blender and blend until smooth.

Pineapple and Coconut Smoothie (serves 1)

Ingredients

110ml/1/2 cup of buttermilk
115g/1 cup of pineapple chunks
1 teaspoon of coconut flakes
1/2 teaspoon coconut extract

Method

Place all ingredients into blender, and process until smooth.

Pineapple and Coconut Smoothie (serves 2)

Ingredients

250g/2 cups cubed/chopped pineapple
1 scoop vanilla ice cream
1/3 small cup of coconut
1 banana
2 medium cups of milk
2 ice cubes

Method

Add all ingredients to the blender. Blend for approximately 30 seconds or until desired consistency. Serve and enjoy immediately.

Pineapple Crush Smoothie (serves 1)

Ingredients

110ml/1/2 cup pineapple juice
4 tablespoons orange juice
90g/3/4 cup melon, roughly chopped
115g/1 cup frozen pineapple chunks
4 ice cubes

Method

Pour the pineapple juice and orange juice into a blender and process gently until combined. Add the melon, pineapple, and ice cubes and process until slushy. Pour into glasses.

Pineapple and Melon Smoothie (serves 2)

Ingredients

1/2 galia melon
4 pineapple rings
1 banana
2 tablespoons of natural yoghurt
5 ice cubes
dash of pineapple juice

Method

Add all ingredients to the blender and put the cubes at the top. Blast for 30 seconds and serve in a long glass with a straw - lovely!

Pineapple and Melon Slush Smoothie (serves 2)

Ingredients

100ml/3 1/3fl oz pineapple juice
4 tablespoon orange juice
125g/1 cup galia melon
140g/1 1/5 cup pineapple chunks
4 crushed ice cubes

Method

Pour the orange and pineapple juice into a food processor and blend together gently until combined. Add the melon, pineapple chunks and ice and blend until it reaches a slushy consistency. Pour into glasses and decorate with slice of orange or pineapple. Serve at once.

Refresher Smoothie (serves 1)

Ingredients

2 good slices of fresh pineapple
2 pears (skin and centre removed)
4 strawberries
splash of juice (either orange or apple)

Method

Add all fruit into the blender and whiz for around 30 seconds. Pour and enjoy.

Tropical Smoothie (serves 2)

Ingredients

200g/1 3/4 cups of orange segments
1 large apple (skin left on but seeds removed)
1 banana sliced
150ml/5fl oz of tropical fruit juice
6 ice cubes

Method

Place all ingredients into a blender and whiz for 30 seconds.

Tropical Delight Smoothie (serves 2)

Ingredients

4 strawberries
1 frozen chopped mango
225ml/1 cup of mango nectar juice
1 frozen chopped banana
1/2 small cup of ice (approx 4 ice cubes)

Method

Put the mango, banana, strawberries, mango nectar and ice in the blender, keep on high until smooth. Pour into glass and enjoy.

Tropical Party Smoothie (serves 8)

Ingredients

3 mangoes
3 papayas
200g/1 3/4 cups frozen mixed berries, defrosted
3 oranges, juiced
2 red grapefruit, juiced

Method

Blend all of the ingredients together until smooth then serve in chilled glasses with ice.

Tropical Tooti Fruity Smoothie (serves 2)

Ingredients

2 bananas
8 strawberries
1 pear
2 kiwi fruits
275ml/1/2 pint of fresh blackcurrant juice

Method

Peel and slice the bananas, cut off the tops of strawberries and cut in half. Peel and de-core the pear and peel and slice the kiwi. Put all fruit including the fresh blackcurrant juice into a blender then blend for approximately 30 seconds until smooth and thick. Serve and enjoy.

Watermelon Wave Smoothie (serves 2)

Ingredients

230g/2 cups of cubed watermelon pieces (fresh or frozen)
115g/1 cup of raspberries
2 scoops of vanilla ice cream

Method

Add fruit to the blender first, blend for approx 20 seconds or until your preferred texture. Next, add the ice cream, blend again for approximately 20 seconds.

Watermelon Margarita Smoothie (serves 2)

Ingredients (Alcoholic)

290g/2 1/2 cups seedless watermelon
3 tablespoons freshly squeezed lime juice
120ml/4 fl oz tequilla
60ml/2 fl oz Cointreau®
450ml/2 cups crushed ice

Method

Cut watermelon into 1 inch cubes, place in blender. Add other ingredients on top with crushed ice last. Blend until smooth. Serve in a decorated cocktail glass.

Create your own tropical and citrus smoothie recipes and write them here:-

Name

Ingredients

Method

Name

Ingredients

Method

Name

Ingredients

Method

Broccoli Smoothie (serves 1)

Ingredients

230g/2 cups of cut raw broccoli
60g/1/2 cup of cut raw green cabbage
1/2 foot of slices of cut raw celery
1 cut peeled apple or 150g/3/4 cup apples juice

Method

Blend all ingredients together until smooth. Add additional liquid (water) to taste.

Broccoli and Grape Smoothie (serves 1)

Ingredients

115g/1 cup of cut raw broccoli
115g/1 cup of red or green grapes (without seeds)
6 crushed ice cubes (optional)

Method

Blend all ingredients together until smooth. Add crushed ice cubes for a fresher taste.

Broccoli and Leek Smoothie (serves 1)

Ingredients

230g/2 cups of cut raw broccoli
230g/2 cups of lightly boiled leeks (less than 8 minutes)
225ml/1 cup of the boiled leek water
115g/1 cup of clean fresh cut raw spinach leaves
60g/1/2 cup of clean fresh cut raw parsley
1/4 spoon turmeric

Method

Blend all ingredients together until smooth. This is a high energy low calorie smoothie.

Carrot Smoothie (serves 2)

Ingredients

3 fresh carrots (peeled & chopped)
cucumber (chopped approx 4 x 2.5cm/1 inch slices)
1 apple (quartered & core removed)
2 handfuls cashew nuts
1/2 handful sunflower seeds
1 small cup fruit juice
3 tablespoons fat-free yoghurt

Method

Place all of the ingredients in the blender and blend until smooth.

Carrot and Nut Smoothie (serves 2)

Ingredients

75g/3oz grated carrots
75g/3oz broccoli
100g/3 3/4oz romaine lettuce
1 lemon
25g/1oz almonds

Method

Blend all ingredients together until smooth.

Carrot and Orange Smoothie (serves 1)

Ingredients

165ml/3/4 cup carrot juice
165ml/3/4 cup orange juice
165ml/3/4 cup vanilla ice cream
6 ice cubes

Method

Pour the carrot juice and orange juice into a blender and process gently until well combined. Add the ice cream and process until thoroughly blended. Add the ice cubes and process until smooth. Pour the mixture into glasses.

Carrot and Spinach Smoothie (serves 1)

Ingredients

230g/2 cups chopped spinach
115g/1 cup chopped carrots
1 banana
225ml/1 cup apple juice
4 ice cubes

Method

Pour the apple juice into a blender. Add the chopped spinach and process until blended. Add the carrots and banana and process well, then add the ice cubes and more juice if necessary.

Carrot and Tomato Smoothie (serves 2)

Ingredients

4 medium sized carrots, cut into 1 inch cubes
6 medium sized tomatoes, quartered
1 stalk celery, chopped into 1/2 inch pieces
1 teaspoon black pepper (freshly grounded)
2 tablespoons fresh lemon juice

Method

Blend all ingredients together, adding additional liquid to taste if necessary.
Pour over crushed ice cubes.

Celery Smoothie (serves 1)

Ingredients

110ml/1/2 cup carrot juice
450g/1 lb tomatoes, skinned, seeded and roughly chopped
1 tablespoon lemon juice
4 celery stalks, trimmed and sliced
4 scallions, trimmed and roughly chopped
60g/1/2 cup roughly chopped fresh parsley
115g/1 cup fresh mint

Method

Put the carrot juice, tomatoes, and lemon juice into a blender and blend gently until combined. Add the sliced celery along with the scallions, parsley, and mint and blend until smooth.

Celery & Kiwi Smoothie (serves 2)

Ingredients

4 very ripe kiwis

1 ripe banana

3 stalks of celery

water

Method

Blend all ingredients until smooth. Add water to taste.

Celery and Strawberry Smoothie (serves 2)

Ingredients

3 sticks of celery

1 medium carton of apple juice

6 strawberries

1 strawberry yoghurt

Method

Chop celery finely and mix individually with the apple juice. Chop and add the strawberries to the mix then blend all the rest of the ingredients together.

Classic Vegetable Smoothie (serves 1)

Ingredients

1 pot plain yoghurt

6 ice cubes

1 small cucumber (peeled and chopped)

1 small tomato

1 chopped celery stalk

3 spinach or romaine leaves

1 tablespoon minced onion (optional)

salt and pepper to taste

Method

Puree all ingredients in a blender, garnish with a cucumber round.

Cucumber and Apple Smoothie (serves 2)

Ingredients

10 good thick slices of cucumber
1 apple

Method

Place the sliced cucumber in the blender, next peel and cut the apple into 4 pieces and add this to the blender. Blend for approx 30 seconds and serve.

Cucumber and Melon Smoothie (serves 1)

Ingredients

60g/1/2 cup chopped cucumber (peeled and seeded, 1/2 inch dice)
175g/1 1/2 cup watermelon, 1 inch cubes
175g/1 1/2 cup cantaloupe, 1 inch cubes
1 pot non fat vanilla yoghurt
8 ice cubes
fresh lime

Method

Place all ingredients together in a blender and mix until smooth. Pour over ice cubes to serve.

Cucumber and Tomato Smoothie (serves 2)

Ingredients

1/2 a small cucumber
1 teaspoon Worcestershire sauce
110ml/1/2 cup tomato juice
6 ice cubes
2 to 3 drops Tabasco sauce

Method

Wash the cucumber and chop roughly. Place in a blender with the Worcestershire sauce, tomato juice, ice cubes and Tabasco sauce.

Peach and Spinach Smoothie (serves 1)

Ingredients

6 peaches, stoned and quartered
2 handfuls of spinach leaves
water

Method

Place all ingredients in a blender and mix until smooth. Add water to taste.

Pumpkin Smoothie (serves 2)

Ingredients

165ml/3/4 cup chilled pumpkin puree
165ml/3/4 cup chilled milk
110ml/1/2 cup vanilla frozen yoghurt
1 tablespoon frozen orange juice concentrate
2 tablespoon sugar
1/4 teaspoon pumpkin pie spice (optional)

Method

Combine all ingredients and blend until combined.

Spicy Spinach Smoothie (serves 2)

Ingredients

1 handful of spinach
335ml/1 1/2 cups water
1 banana
1 mango
1/4 teaspoon cayenne pepper

Method

Blend all ingredients together until smooth, adding water to create the desired consistency.

Spinach and Cashew Nut Smoothie (serves 1)

Ingredients

225g/8oz mixed fruit, frozen
110g/4oz baby spinach
165ml3/4 cup white grape juice
55ml/1/4 cup water
50g/2oz cashews

Method

Blend all ingredients together until smooth.

Spicy Vegetable Smoothie (serves 2)

Ingredients

450ml/2 cups tomato juice
60g/1/2 cup chopped red bell pepper
60g/1/2 cup peeled and chopped cucumber
3 teaspoon lemon juice
2 teaspoon chopped scallions
2 teaspoon Worcestershire sauce
1/4 teaspoon salt
1/4 teaspoon fresh ground pepper
1/4 teaspoon hot pepper sauce

Method

Combine all ingredients in a blender and process until smooth - about 3 minutes. Chill for approx 30 minutes before serving.

Tomato Lemon Twist Smoothie (serves 1)

Ingredients

2 tomatoes, cut in chunks
1 cup tomato juice (or 2-3 medium tomatoes, juiced)
1/2 lemon, juiced
1 teaspoon freshly grated lemon rind
6 fresh basil leaves, rinsed

Method

Blend all ingredients on high speed and serve over crushed ice. Add black pepper to taste.

Create your own vegetable smoothie recipes and write them here:-

Name

Ingredients

Method

Name

Ingredients

Method

Name

Ingredients

Method

We all know the health benefits of including fruit and vegetables into our diet, so try these tasty juices as a lighter alternative.

Blueberry Cherry Juice

Ingredients

handful of cherries, pitted
90g/3/4 cup blueberries
1 apple, cored and sliced

Method

Process through a juicer and serve.

Citrus Burst

Ingredients

1/2 red grapefruit, deseeded and sectioned
1 orange, peeled and sectioned
2 handfuls cranberries

Method

Process through a juicer and serve.

Fruit Juice Punch

Ingredients

6 strawberries, fresh or thawed from frozen
1 apple, cored and sliced
1/2 orange, peeled and sectioned

Method

Process through a juicer and serve.

Fruit Nectar

Ingredients

60g/1/2 cup raspberries, fresh or thawed from frozen
1 orange, peeled and sectioned
1 nectarine, pitted and sliced

Method

Process through a juicer and serve.

Gingered Apple Cider Juice

Ingredients

2.5cm/1 inch piece ginger

3 apples or 225ml/1 cup apple juice

Method

Process through a juicer and serve.

Lemon~Lime Ginger Ale

Ingredients

handful of grapes (stems off)

1 apple, cored and sliced

2.5cm/1/2 inch fresh ginger (optional)

1/2 lime

1/4 lemon

sparkling mineral water

Method

Juice the apple and ginger together, then juice the rest of the fruit, pour in a large glass and fill to the top with sparkling water and serve with ice.

Orange Boost

Ingredients

2 oranges, peeled and sectioned

1 mango, peeled and sliced

1 apple, cored and sliced

Method

Process through a juicer and serve.

Peach Pear Apple Juice

Ingredients

1 apple, cored and sliced

2 peaches, remove seed

1 pear, sliced

Method

Process through a juicer and serve.

Peachy Pear Juice

Ingredients

1 pear, peeled and quartered

1 peach, peeled and stoned

1 apple, cored and sliced

Method

Process through a juicer and serve.

Sparkling Tropical Fruit Juice

Ingredients

1 kiwi, peeled

1 orange, peeled and sectioned

1/2 mango, peeled and sliced

sparkling mineral water

Method

Process the fruit in a juicer. Pour the juice in a large glass and fill to the top with sparkling water and serve.

Strawberry and Apple Juice

Ingredients

1 cup strawberries, chopped

2 med. apples, cored and sliced

1 teaspoon lemon juice

Method

Process through a juicer and serve.

Strawberry and Pineapple Juice

Ingredients

115g/1 cup strawberries, chopped

1/2 fresh pineapple cored and sliced

1 teaspoon lemon juice

Method

Process through a juicer and serve.

Create your own juice recipes and write them here:-

Name

Ingredients

Method

Name

Ingredients

Method

Name

Ingredients

Method

INDEX

Cc

Mm

Yy